Growing Up, B

George C. Marshal

Uniontown, Pennsylvania - Lexington,

1880-1901

Written by Mary Sutton Skutt
with
Illustrations by Robert Tharp

Printed by The News-Gazette
Lexington, Virginia
1997

George C. Marshall
1880 - 1959

This is my first published book, and I dedicate it to my husband Dick Skutt, our children Jim, Kathy, Barbara and Glenn, their spouses, and all of our grandchildren along with my love, always. Mary -- a.k.a. Mom and Grandma Mary

P E N N S Y L V A N I A

Curwensville · Tyrone · Lewistown · Sunbury · Shenandoah · Tamaqua · Mauch Chu·

STOWN · Altoona · Huntingdon · Ashland · Allentown · Belvi· · Easto·

Hills · Bedford · Gettysburg · Harrisburg · Reading · PHILADELPHIA

S · T · CUMBERLAND · GREEN SPRING · Chambersburg · VAL. · Lancaster · Columbia · LANDENBURG · Chester

Paw Paw · R Johns Run · HANCOCK · Cherry Run · Martinsburg · Kernsville · Shenandoah Jc. · HAGERSTOWN · Susquehanna · York · Brandywine Springs · WILM·

Berkeley Spring · Charlestown · Wadesville · Stephenson · Antietam · WEVERTON · Brunswick · WASHINGTON JC. · FREDERICK · Frederick · Mount Air · RELAY · BALTIMORE · Aberdeen · Havre de Grace · Dover

WINCHESTER · Kernstown · Middletown · apon Road · SBURG · JC. · Rock · B. & W. R.D. · O. HARPERS FERRY · Gaithersburg · Rockville · Forest Glen · WASHINGTON · Laurel · Annapolis Jc. · Annapolis · PATUXENT · BAY · Centerville · Oxford

Riverton · RY. P. · Alexandria · Shepherd · CHESAPEAKE · Cambridge

Manassas · SOU · & · ALEXANDRIA · Brandywine · D.

Warrenton · Quantico · Popes Creek · M. · Salisbury · Ber·

Luray · Culpeper · Washington B. Co. · Crisfield · Fran·Ci·

Orange · Gordonsville · P. F. & P. · Fredericksburg & · NORFOLK & WASHINGTON S.B. CO. · A.

Charlottesville · OHIO · R. · Milford · Rappahannock R. · I.

Columbia & · CHIO · Doswell · N. · Cape Charles

James · Richmond · West Point · Yorktown · York R.

Amelia C.H. · Manchester · RY. · C. & · OLD POINT COMFORT

Petersburg · River · Claremont · NEWPORT NEWS

Burkeville · Waverly · PORTSMOUTH · NORFOLK

Keysville · Notto·

ACKNOWLEDGMENTS

Thanks to my husband for having infinite patience and understanding as well as reading the first and final drafts, sharing the computer, and fixing our meals when I forgot. This book would not have happened without your support. You helped me to "enjoy the process" so, sincerely, I thank you.

I thank my encouraging and supportive friends at the George C. Marshall Library and Museum and also at the Virginia Military Institute Archives. They loaned me the books and found the files from which I gathered all the anecdotes, quotations, pictures, and facts. Everyone was ever helpful and enthusiastic about my project and I appreciate it. A special thanks to Jeanne Pedersen, of the Marshall Foundation staff, for designing the book cover.

I especially thank Marti Gansz, the Assistant to the Archivist/Librarian of the Marshall Library, for her many hours (days) of friendly and efficient help. She located the picture of the Cub Scouts with Secretary Marshall and even helped me to locate some of those 1948 boys.

Thanks to Tom Camden, Director of the George C. Marshall Archives and Library and to C.J. Roberts, Director of the George C. Marshall Museum, for their kind assistance and their interest, as in, "How's the book coming along?" week after week after week. Karen Vest, a Marshall Library summer apprentice, helped me to organize and transport the Marshall photo collection.

Diane Jacob, Virginia Military Institute Archivist, was especially helpful with many early photos, post cards, invitations and announcements of the time. I thank her also for suggesting I should read Henry Fry's memoirs!

Thanks to all of the manuscript readers -- Dara Ann Babbitt, Chip Barnett, Fred Hadsel, Kit Huffman, Martha Mehler, Marilyn Pearson, Hart Slater, Jeri Watts, Pat Thomas -- all of whom made valuable suggestions for improvements.

Many, many thanks to Robert Tharp, the artist, who even sketched while on vacation! Thanks to Jim Dedrick, of The News Gazette, for his steady guidance and who kept smiling and telling me, "It's going to happen!" Thanks to Gay Lea Goodbar for typesetting and lay-out, putting up with my mistakes and "just a few more changes."

This was a first-time experience, I enjoyed every bit of it, and I couldn't have done it alone. Thanks, everyone.

MSS

George C. Marshall at home in Uniontown, PA at age 16.

GROWING UP, BY GEORGE!
George C. Marshall's early years
Uniontown, Pennsylvania-Lexington, Virginia
1880-1901

CONTENTS

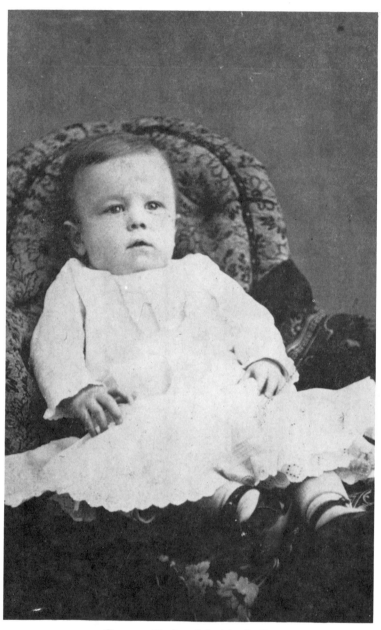

George Catlett Marshall, Jr.

CHAPTER 1

GEORGE PICKS THE PIRATE

George C. Marshall hated to be last. Whenever he was last, he thought it was his fault and that he had failed. In his life's first adventure---being born---it wasn't anybody's fault and he didn't fail, but he *was* last!

Also, it was the very last day of December in 1880 when George C. Marshall, Jr. was born in Uniontown, Pennsylvania. George was named for his father and was the youngest child of George Catlett Marshall and Laura Emily Bradford Marshall. When he was born, his brother Stuart was almost six years old and his sister Marie was four.

December 31, 1880, and New Year's Eve in Uniontown was probably quiet and very dark except for home-made music, firecrackers, oil lamps or gas lights. Exactly one year before on December 31, Thomas A. Edison had received a patent for his invention of the light bulb. Electricity, as we know it, in the home or city, did not exist.

There were no telephones, movies, televisions or computers. Airplanes, cars, trucks, buses, motorcycles and space shuttles did not exist. But there were trains and ships, factories and homes. They all needed coal to burn to make steam for power and heat.

The coal industry offered promising job opportunities to Mr. Marshall after the Civil War. He moved his family from Augusta, Kentucky to Uniontown, Pennsylvania where he had found a good job in one of the coal companies.

Many people in America were busy trying to put their families, their homes, and their work lives back together after that terrible time of trouble and death, known as The Civil War. Many families had argued and split in siding with the North or the South.

The Marshall Family of Uniontown, PA

George Catlett Marshall, Sr.
Born 1845

Laura Bradford Marshall
Born 1846

Marie Louise
Born 1876

Stuart Bradford
Born 1875

George Catlett
Born 1880

Ancestors of George Catlett Marshall, Jr.

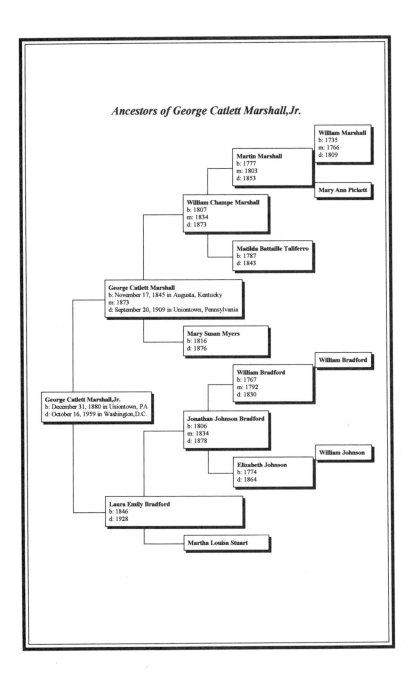

William Marshall
b: 1735
m: 1766
d: 1809

Martin Marshall
b: 1777
m: 1803
d: 1853

Mary Ann Pickett

William Champe Marshall
b: 1807
m: 1834
d: 1873

Matilda Battaille Taliferro
b: 1787
d: 1843

George Catlett Marshall
b: November 17, 1845 in Augusta, Kentucky
m: 1873
d: September 20, 1909 in Uniontown, Pennsylvania

Mary Susan Myers
b: 1816
d: 1876

William Bradford

William Bradford
b: 1767
m: 1792
d: 1830

George Catlett Marshall, Jr.
b: December 31, 1880 in Uniontown, PA
d: October 16, 1959 in Washington, D.C.

Jonathan Johnson Bradford
b: 1806
m: 1834
d: 1878

William Johnson

Elizabeth Johnson
b: 1774
d: 1864

Laura Emily Bradford
b: 1846
d: 1928

Martha Louisa Stuart

George C. Marshall
(Age 2)

4

George C. Marshall
(Age 5)

5

At the age of sixteen, Mr. Marshall had been in the Union militia, known as the Home Guard. He had even been a prisoner of the Confederates for a few days. And the unit that captured him was led by one of his distant Southern cousins!

Two of Mr. Marshall's brothers fought in Lee's Army, for the South. A more distant relative, Colonel Charles Marshall, was an aide to General Robert E. Lee and carefully wrote, as Gen. Lee dictated, his last field order---- his farewell address in April of 1865.

Although they came from Kentucky, and lived in Pennsylvania, the Marshall family was strongly connected to Virginia in its heritage. Many of their ancestors came from there. There were several lawyers on the Marshall side of the family. Supreme Court Chief Justice, John Marshall, was a first cousin to George's great-grandfather.

The Bradford side of the family boasted of several doctors, including Mrs. Marshall's father. The family was proud of its genealogy and, at an early age, his parents taught George about his ancestors. George was not impressed.

But one day, while reading in a book of family history, he found a story claiming Blackbeard the Pirate had married one of his Marshall ancestors. A pirate in the family? Jolly Good! George was impressed.

George liked the idea of having a pirate as one of his ancestors.

He took the book out and around, showing it off to his friends. George C. Marshall, Jr. proudly announced that his father was descended from Blackbeard . . .

". . . a pirate who had a very bloody and cruel history and a long beard to help out . . . " ; . . . a terrible rogue who was hung for his crimes!

His friends were impressed. His father was *not* impressed!

"Father was perfectly furious . . . that I had publicized him in. . . . town for being descended . . .from a pirate."

Years later, and after he had heard much too often about Chief Justice John Marshall and his thirty-four years in the United States Supreme Court, George Marshall made this comment:

"I thought that the continual harping on the name of John Marshall was kind of poor business. It was about time for somebody else to swim for the family."

George C. Marshall, Jr. may have been the last born in his family, but he became a first in other ways. He had a more impressive life than any pirate hero he could pick, and his life of adventure began in Uniontown, Pennsylvania.

CHAPTER 2

OUT AND ABOUT WITH GEORGE

The Marshall family rented a two-story, ivy-clad, brick house on the edge of town at the end of West Main Street. Close to the house was a small barn, a fruit orchard, and a creek called Coal Lick Run. George had plenty of time for adventure.

General Marshall said, " . . .my first very clear recollection is going out to our barn in which we kept a horse and a cow."

One day he followed his brother to the stable. Stuart went quickly up the wooden ladder to the hay loft, and George followed, for his first climb. Going slowly and carefully, one rough board after another, he came upon a window-like opening.

He could look down on the chickens wandering in the barnyard, and on Coal Lick Run with the ducks swimming about and dogs playing on the creek bank. Everything appeared small and different.

"All of it fascinated me, and it seemed a whole world exposed in an instant to my eye."

Since Stuart was about six years older, there wasn't much contact or affection between George and his brother. Usually Stuart didn't include George in his playing or his plans but, now and then, Stuart had no choice except to put up with his brother.

The National Guard set up camp one summer's night near George's house and, ". . . all of the boys immediately became very military." Stuart and his friends set up a gunny sack (burlap) tent across Coal Lick Run to camp out for the night.

George was about six years old and he wanted to camp, too. And their mother saw to it that Stuart took him. The older boys were not at all happy to have such a little kid along on such an important adventure.

The big boys had crossbow guns to put on their shoulders. They made a track in front of the tent, numbered themselves off, . . .1 . . .2. . .3 and then took turns guarding the tent. Number One, ". . . walked his post and called out, 'Number One and all is well.'"

As it got dark, George got sleepy. He went inside the tent and the older boys, glad to be rid of him, happily continued with their army play.

Suddenly the camp was under attack! Something large and dark came towards them and their tent! A low moaning, deep breathing and slow, heavy footsteps came with it.

In the blackness and amid the excitement, " . . .the garrison fled. . .," forgetting all about little George. They fell down the high creek bank and ran for home.

A dripping wet Stuart had no idea what to say when his mother asked about George.

"My father. . . made . . . Stuart lead the way . . . while they recovered me and saved my life . . ." But much to Stuart's dismay, ". . . they found me fast asleep."

George missed out on "the great military adventure," and the non-attack of the neighbor's <u>cow!</u>

His sister, Marie, thought George was a pest more than anything else. Marie claimed that George was so aggravating she wondered how she ever got married. She said that when boys came to call on her, George dropped water bombs on their heads from the upstairs window. Teasing Marie was one of his favorite sports.

Another favorite sport of George and his buddies was bee fighting. One summer day Marie had a party for a friend, the daughter of the Pennsylvania governor. Marie asked that her "barbarian brother" not be allowed in the house during the party. So George went to his friend's house where they decided to do some bee fighting.

To do good bee fighting, they bored air holes through wooden shingles which helped the shingles swing faster. Then they found a bee nest. The object of the game was to stir up the bees, make them really mad, hit at them like crazy with the shingle, and keep from getting stung.

What a sport! That party day one bee became set on stinging George. The bee was fast and the bee was mad! George high-tailed it for home.

"My front door was open and I went straight down the long hall. Then I remembered I was forbidden in the house. The party was going on . . . peaceful and delightful . . .at the last moment I turned . . .into the dining room. But the bee went straight ahead and stung the guest of honor."

Marie would sometimes tease George to get back at him for teasing her, as sisters often do to pesky younger brothers.

One day, George was using the water hose to clean the paved street in front of their house. Horses pulled the trolley, wagons, and buggies along West Main Street in Uniontown then, and washing the street was a chore that had to be done every day because of the horses. It was not a difficult chore, but it was a necessary one.

George did it because his father ordered it done, but he hated doing it. Other children would make remarks as they passed by on their way to school. The girls would snicker and giggle as they went by, and that was bad enough, but on that particular morning,

". . .Marie was laughing and jeering from the upstairs window."

That was just too much! George made a decision. As he was finishing with the hosing, he heard the front door close. Could he get Marie? He whirled around and caught her full blast with the hose.

But it wasn't Marie he hit. It was his mother!

Mrs. Marshall wiped away the water, straightened her glasses and was,

". . . . rather shocked but much amused because she knew the terrible plight I was in."

Part of that terrible plight came from George's father, who was not one bit amused. Spankings, whippings or "lickings" were a part of home and school discipline in those days. Many parents thought, "spare the rod and spoil the child."

George "took a licking" frequently for doing what his father thought was wrong. He had played hooky from school once and spent the day at Gadd's blacksmith shop. Marie found him there and told their father. George C. Marshall, Jr. got a licking on that day, indeed!

14

But it wasn't Marie he hit. It was his mother!

His father was very strict with George, and George tried hard to win his father's approval. Sometimes he did and sometimes he didn't. On the morning that he squirted his mother, Mr. Marshall gave George, Jr. the last whipping General Marshall could remember getting.

George's mother usually knew of his mischief, but not his father. He only told his father about his successes. Any trouble he got into, he saved for telling his mother. His mother protected him and spoiled him a bit. Sometimes she even laughed at his escapades.

"I told her everything I did, and she never corrected me. Because if I told her, I realized it was wrong (and) there was no use telling me again it was wrong. . . she had quite a sense of humor . . ."

George and his father got along well, though, when it came to history and hunting. The older George would tell exciting tales of battles and explorers to the younger George as they hunted and fished in the same places where George Washington built his first fort and fought his first battle in 1754. The roadway called The National Pike, connecting Baltimore to the West, ran right past their house. George Washington had traveled along that road.

Young George liked hearing about George Washington, the French and Indian War, the Louis and Clark expedition and, of course, the Civil War. He soaked up history like a sponge soaks up water, and he remembered for always those stories his father told.

Mr. Marshall liked to hunt. He was an excellent shot and taught George about guns and shooting grouse and quail. So George enjoyed hunting. His father also liked to fish. He taught George about the streams and bait and how to catch bass. George, Jr. liked fishing.

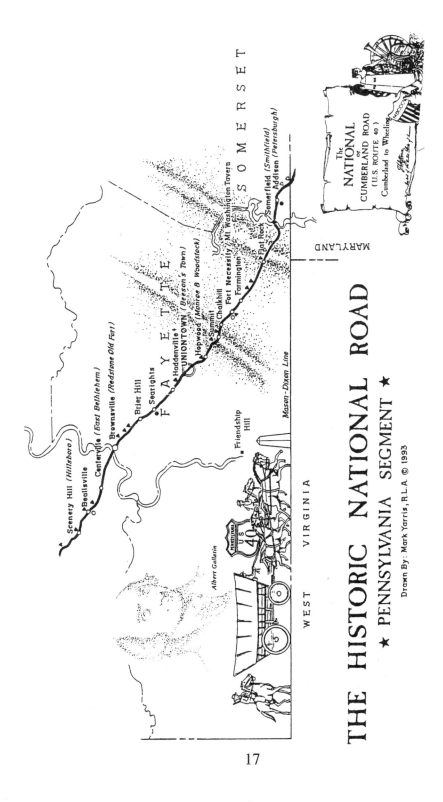

THE HISTORIC NATIONAL ROAD

★ PENNSYLVANIA SEGMENT ★

Drawn By: Mark Yarris, R.L.A. © 1993

17

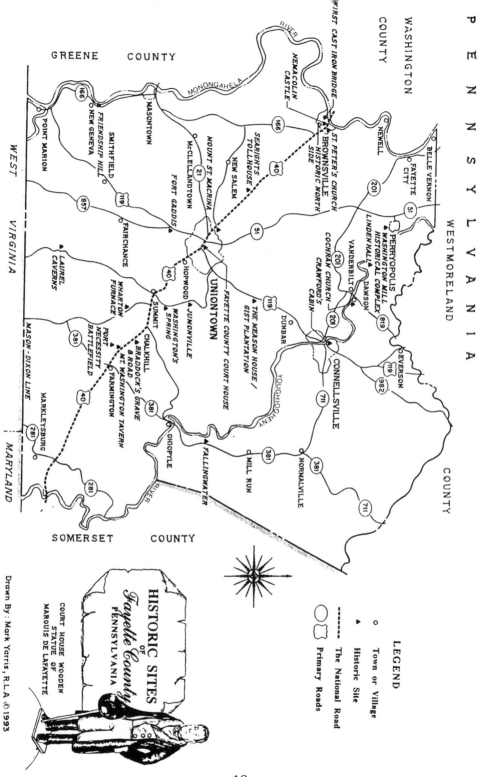

HISTORIC SITES
OF
Fayette County
PENNSYLVANIA

COURT HOUSE WOODEN
STATUE OF
MARQUIS DE LAFAYETTE

Drawn By: Mark Yarris, R.L.A. © 1993

WEST VIRGINIA

MASON-DIXON LINE

MARYLAND

SOMERSET   COUNTY

GREENE   COUNTY

MONONGAHELA   RIVER

FIRST CAST IRON BRIDGE

NEMACOLIN CASTLE

POINT MARION

NEW GENEVA

FRIENDSHIP HILL

SMITHFIELD

MASONTOWN

McCLELLANDTOWN

MOUNT ST. MACRINA

FORT GADDIS

FAIRCHANCE

NEW SALEM

SEARIGHTS TOLLHOUSE

ST. PETER'S CHURCH

BROWNSVILLE HISTORIC NORTH SIDE

BELLE VERNON

NEWELL

FAYETTE CITY

PERRYOPOLIS

WASHINGTON MILL HISTORICAL COMPLEX

LINDEN HALL

COCHRAN CHURCH

CRAWFORD'S CRAWFORD'S CABIN

VANDERBILT

DAWSON

LAUREL CAVERNS

WHARTON FURNACE

HOPWOOD

UNIONTOWN

FAYETTE COUNTY COURT HOUSE

THE MEASON HOUSE / GIST PLANTATION

DUNBAR

YOUGHIOGHENY

CONNELLSVILLE

EVERSON

SUMMIT

JUMONVILLE

WASHINGTON'S SPRING

CHALKHILL

BRADDOCK'S GRAVE & ROAD

MT. WASHINGTON TAVERN

FORT NECESSITY BATTLEFIELD

FARMINGTON

MARKLEYSBURG

OHIOPYLE

RIVER

FALLINGWATER

MILL RUN

NORMALVILLE

HISTORIC SITES

LEGEND

○   Town or Village

▲   Historic Site

------   The National Road

◯   Primary Roads

One day his father went fishing with two friends and they took George along. After fishing all morning and catching nothing, the two friends decided to go further upstream. The creek bank was rocky and the going was too rough for a small boy.

Mr. Marshall told the others to go ahead and that he would stay behind with his son. He and George would just fish from where they were. George could tell his father was disappointed.

His father hadn't given him a real fishing rod because he didn't think George was big enough to handle one. But George didn't give up trying to catch a fish. A large flat rock hung out over the creek and the boy dangled his fishing line, with a double hook, below the rock and into the shade.

Suddenly, he had a bite! When his father helped him bring in the line, there wasn't one fish on it. There were two---one on each hook!

As fast as they could bait their hooks and drop them in the water, they caught a fish! That evening back at camp, they met the other two men who still had caught nothing all day long. The two George C. Marshalls stood together, side by side, and calmly showed off their own thirty fish.

George C. Marshall learned by listening and by doing, but he also learned a lot by reading. Books were important in George Marshall's family.

At night, his father read to the family the books and stories by James Fenimore Cooper and other popular writers of the 1890s. Those books were long and heavy reading and George remembered parts of them all of his life.

"In my home life, . . . I got a great deal of benefit from reading. My father read aloud, very well, and liked to do it, strange to say. He read a great many things. . . and I remember them today very clearly and it is a delightful recollection."

George was strongly encouraged to read books his parents read, but was forbidden to read any of the Nick Carter adventure books.

His parents did not consider 'penny novels' to be 'good literature' for children. That only caused George to read all the Nick Carter books he could find, on the sly! And reading Nick Carter got him into trouble at church.

The Marshall family were active members of St. Peter's Episcopal Church in Uniontown. At that time, church organs needed to have air pumped through them in order to make music. Someone had to "...pull the bellows," or pump the organ, by hand.

"I pumped the organ ...and the place for the pumper was in a very narrow region in rear of the organ...and the pump was just a handle like...the tiller of a boat."

The pumping was not difficult, but he did have to be there and be alert. Sometimes the preacher's sermon seemed endless. George couldn't see him so it was hard to stay interested.

"... there was a long period of wait during the sermon. And on one of these mornings I was occupying the period of waiting by reading a five-cent novel of that day about Nick Carter. Just in the most exciting portion ... it was very much like Jesse James...I realized that she had started to play ... and there was no music coming out. So I pumped the organ very hurriedly."

But he wasn't fast enough!

The organist was not only displeased, she was furious. George C. Marshall, Jr. was relieved of his duty as an organ pumper that very moment.

George liked attending church and went regularly with his parents. He was more religious than some boys, reading the Bible every day and saying his prayers on his knees at night, but that's the way he was taught to do. His parents had him christened on June 5, 1881, at St. Peter's and he was confirmed there on February 7, 1896, when he was fifteen years old. Still, being religious didn't make a saint out of George!

At home, Mrs. Marshall played the piano quite well and had a pleasant singing voice. George's father had a fine tenor voice and liked to sing with her. Stuart could play several instruments and both he and Marie could sing. George did not play and could not sing.

All he could do during the family sing-alongs was to, ". . .sit around on a hassock and listen and keep quiet. . . . " And that was difficult for George to do for long. He would rather be on the look-out for adventure.

CHAPTER 3

NOW PLAYING -
THE ADVENTURES OF GEORGE AND ANDY

Across the street from the Marshalls, in a brick house built just like theirs, lived Andy Thompson. George and Andy were the same age and best friends. The boys played together throughout childhood and into their teens remaining good friends even after they were grown, and sometimes talked of their exciting adventures as youngsters. Herb Bowman, Jim Conrad, Billy Ewing, Alex Mead, Bill Wood were among the boys that George C. Marshall called his friends.

Uniontown was a busy town. George and his friends went all around it, visiting the storekeepers, the blacksmith, the barber shop and the baseball field. They knew the town well.

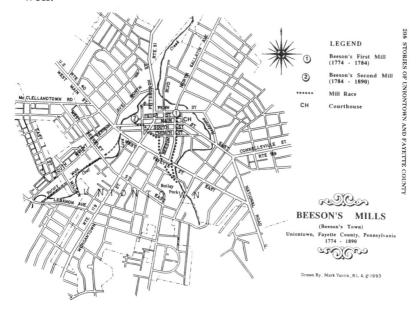

LEGEND

① Beeson's First Mill (1774 - 1784)

② Beeson's Second Mill (1784 - 1890)

•••••• Mill Race

CH Courthouse

BEESON'S MILLS
(Beeson's Town)
Uniontown, Fayette County, Pennsylvania
1774 - 1890

Drawn By: Mark Yarris, RLA © 1993

"The town . . . was very simple and very attractive. . . a boyhood recollection of a place like that is rather difficult to compare to modern recollections. But I always thought it was a charming place to live and we had great fun out of it . . . largely centered around our yard which was fairly large. And the creek, of course, which was the great jewel of the production."

George C. Marshall had a snub nose, freckles and blue eyes. His friends nicknamed him 'Flicker' for his sandy colored hair. He stayed with his little group of close friends and would rather play soldier than baseball. His favorite play clothes included black cotton shirts. They kept his mother from knowing how dirty his neck was.

With his friends, he liked a good joke, liked excitement, planning and making things. He didn't have much to say, but sometimes he was daring.

A tree branch with a rope tied on it gave him a chance to show off once. George climbed into the tree, grabbed the rope, and pushed off and away from the tree.

He heard "Ooohhs" and he heard "ahhhhs." Yes! the neighborhood girls were watching!

So he went higher and higher, doing tricks like an acrobat in the circus.

Suddenly Flicker shot off the rope, flew through the air and landed in the Thompsons' bean patch, just beyond their picket fence.

Whew-eee! he was lucky. He only left the seat of his pants on one of the fence's pointed posts!

Once, in the Thompsons' yard, about twenty feet from their wash house, where every week's washing was done beneath the tree George had swung from on the rope, he and Andy found an ant parade. They sprawled belly-down and watched.

". . . there was a deep trail---you could rest your thumb in it---and a continuous procession of ants going and coming to the tree or to the wash house and those going one direction would generally carry some little white burden. . . . Well, we would lie and watch those ants by the hour when we had nothing else to do. . . we would watch this ant procession."

It was difficult for the boys to believe the ants could survive the annual spring flooding of Coal Lick Run when the entire yard would be under two feet of water, but they did. After every flood, the ant parade began again.

George followed the ants with his thumb.

In 1939, General Marshall visited Uniontown, and he went to the site of the famous ant procession he had known as a boy.

"I was very curious about the trail of the ants and I went down to this house . . .but I couldn't find the trail. The spring house, of course, was gone. But the honey locust was still standing. . . ."

An old man was sitting in a rocking chair watching him, and General Marshall told him he was looking for the ant trail and asked the man if he had ever seen it. The man knew exactly where it was.

". . . And he said I was turned around as to location of the wash house. He pointed it out   where it really was, and I went out there and I immediately found the trail of ants running exactly as it had in my boyhood so many, many years before."

George and Andy tried to save the town from bandits when they were about eight years old. That spring a group of robbers had broken into several homes in the area and taken the stolen goods off into the hills. The law officials had caught them, but George and Andy were inspired with the thought of ambushing possible outlaws. They armed themselves with air rifles and took to the hills, near the road.

When a farmer went driving by, they would jump out from their hiding place, after the wagon or buggy had passed, and fire BBs at him. They didn't aim to hit anyone. But one day a BB pellet went through the open window in the back of a buggy and struck a farmer in the back of the neck.

Luckily, little boys can run faster than some farmers! They escaped, but they were afraid to be seen going home. So they turned their coats wrong side out and their hats around backwards and thought nobody would know them..

"My mother thought that was the funniest thing she ever saw when we turned up in this 'disguise'."

His mother protected George, for two or three days, from answering the embarrassing questions that would have identified him as one of the ambushers. Both boys were afraid to leave their homes during those days and that was punishment enough. That ended George Marshall's outlaw career.

Beyond their houses on the edge of town, the National Road went over a bridge and disappeared over the next few hills. In between the hills were the valleys, which the local people called hollows. To George and Andy, adventure must be waiting just for them over those hills and in those hollows.

At about the age of ten, Flicker and Andy went on an exploration of the 'third hollow'. From their earliest days, the boys had been told there were three hollows beyond the high hill that overlooked their houses at the end of Main Street.

When they were very little they had gone to the 'first hollow', and a few years later they went over to the 'second hollow'. But they had never before dared to go to the 'third hollow'.

For such a long trip they had to carry supplies. Mrs. Marshall was let in on their plan and helped them pack some food---bread and jam sandwiches, boiled sweet potatoes and a jar of milk.

The boys also took along their rubber guns (we call them sling shots) and some pellets. They left home around four o'clock in the morning, and when it got light, they "shot at everything that hopped but didn't hit anything."

In the 'first hollow', they ate their lunch. In the 'second hollow' they ate dinner. And when they reached that 'third hollow' they finished off the leftovers and started home.

They hurried. They were sure that nightfall would bring out the wild beasts that roamed around the hollows. Finally they were home again and they rushed inside.

The Marshall family was at the dining room table. Eating breakfast! George and Andy felt as if they had "achieved the North Pole," although they had only been gone for a few hours.

George and Andy spent a great deal of their time trying to earn money. A few extra pennies here and there meant they could go to the circus or to the state fair. That often made for exciting adventure in the springtime.

CHAPTER 4
HOW'S BUSINESS, GEORGE C. ?

Saturday afternoons were busy times for George and Andy. They had headquarters in the barn behind Andy's house where they organized shows and circuses. Their friends and patrons (neighborhood children or parents) paid two or three cents admission. In warm weather, they bought powdered licorice at the candy store, mixed it with water and sold it for one or two cents a glass at their cold drink stand near the street.

With the profits from these ventures, they could go off into town to Kramer's store where they might spend a penny or two of their hard-earned money on goodies for themselves. Or maybe they went to the circus or to the fair.

"I arrived at the circus train, watched it unload, and got out to the circus. My main occupation was getting in without paying for it."

One of the exciting events of the year for George and Andy was the state fair. It might not have been the real state fair, but that was what it was called. The boys liked to go while the fair was setting up and see how the mid-way games of chance were fixed, how the men could control who won the prizes. ·

A favorite trick of the boys was to buy a half-price ticket, go through the gate, get inside a tent and into the stands, and then crawl out under the back of the tent. They resold their ticket for full price and crawled back in, with money to spend.

Mr. Marshall caught George doing this once and gave him quite a strong tongue lashing. George didn't do that again!

In the early spring, Coal Lick Run would overflow and the Marshall's garden, yard and the basement of the house would flood. Because of the richness of their soil from the wash-offs, the Marshalls' vegetable garden was often the best in town.

After visiting the real greenhouses on the outskirts of town with their mothers, George and Andy decided to open a greenhouse. The boys figured they could make money selling plants, too, if only they had a greenhouse.

In the Marshalls' backyard, there was an old tool shed. They went to the local carriage shop owner and asked for his leftover paint. George and Andy painted the shed, as high as they could reach and as long as the paint lasted, green. Then they had a "greenhouse."

A flag was made out of white material and they wrote on it "Marshall & Thompson," and below that they wrote, "Florists" ---- only they left out the L, so it was "Forists". They hoped no one would notice and hung it on their "greenhouse."

Into tin cans, they put barnyard soil and plants they dug from their yards. It wasn't long before they had a fine crop of strong and healthy --- weeds, marked 'For Sale'.

The girls from school were their best customers, buying up "growing green things" for a few pennies.

George and Andy potted some dainty, pale blue flowers into old strawberry baskets which they had painted green with a black stripe. The girls happily paid several pennies for the "lovely and rare flowers."

They were not one bit happy when they found those same type of flowers, called Forget-me-nots, blooming wild in the woods. From the holes in the ground, they knew then exactly where the boys had gotten their "lovely, rare flowers"! The boys' greenhouse business wilted.

31

Later on George and Andy heard the government would give free seeds to anyone who wrote their congressman requesting them. Quickly they wrote to a Pennsylvania congressman, and sure enough, they received a package of free seed--- cotton seed. Too bad cotton does not grow in Pennsylvania.

In the fall and winter, they had a restaurant of sorts in the lean-to at the old spring house in the Marshalls' back yard. They had a serving counter and an old stove that still worked.

Andy was the cook and wore a chef's hat made from newspaper. George was the waiter and called out the orders in a very loud voice. They sold apples and sweet potatoes cooked in the stove and made tasty with lots of sugar sprinkled on them from a red-handled, tin shaker.

One day their customers came as usual, but suddenly refused to buy. They claimed the sweet potatoes were no good. George consulted Andy. The restaurant was out of sugar, so he had filled the shaker with sand. That put a gritty end to the restaurant venture.

George and Andy were resourceful when it came to earning money. Once they set up a bar in the Marshalls' basement and sold corn-silk cigars and root beer. The root beer belonged to Mr. Marshall. He had made it and put it there about six months earlier. It tasted so terrible nobody could drink it.

When George and Andy discovered the beer, it tasted fine to them. In fact, it was good enough to sell!

"We had the whole town in our cellar. Our father came home one day and found this affair going on full speed. . . he sampled the root beer and then seized the whole issue . . ." and the bartending business dried up!

Mr. Marshall had the stable behind their house torn down, so George and Andy took some boards and tried to build a boat. Their boards were too thick and too heavy. A brother of the local toy store owner came to the rescue with better materials and they soon had a fine flat bottom boat. It became the local ferry.

Coal Lick Run was their 'river' and wasn't much wider than the boat, but the ferry let other children, especially girls, take a short cut to and from school. Andy Thompson was the engineer and steered the boat.

George was the conductor. He printed tickets on his toy typewriter, put his hat on backwards and sold those tickets to the girls, for pennies or pins. Then Andy poled the craft across the creek and George took up the tickets as a real conductor should.

One day some girls refused to give up their tickets. Andy began laughing. The girls giggled and made fun of George. That put George in a tough spot. He hated for Andy to laugh at him, let alone the girls! He had to think fast.

He looked down. In the bottom of the boat was a drain and the drain was plugged with a cork. George pulled out the cork. Water shot up through the hole, quickly flooding the boat. And it sank!

George pulled the plug and sank the boat.

The water was no more than two feet deep, but the girls were drenched. Everybody had to wade to shore. Naturally, the girls told their parents what had happened. Their ferry business went under.

George took another "licking" from his father for pulling such a trick, but he felt his solution was worth the scolding.

"I never forgot that . . . because I had to do something, and I had to think quickly, and what I did set me up again as the temporary master of the situation."

But being master of a situation didn't follow George Marshall to school.

CHAPTER 5

THE STUDENT WHO WASN'T ONE

School was not a happy part of George Marshall's childhood. When he was five, his mother's elderly aunt lived with the family. She was very smart and thought George should begin studying early. She sat him in front of her and had him repeat his lessons for hours. That was torture! George could see and hear his friends playing outside.

"She so soured me on study and teaching that I liked never to have recovered from it."

At age six he went to Miss Alcinda Thompson's private school which met in a small, white, clapboard building on Church Street in Uniontown. After learning to hate studying to begin with, he was happy to find he didn't have to do much of it at Miss Thompson's school.

The best part of Miss Thompson's school for George was recess. He wasn't one to talk much, but at recess he would line up the children, give them stick 'guns' to carry on their shoulders, and march them around the schoolyard. He liked to play soldier. He liked giving the orders. In playing at war, he was a leader.

In the classroom, he was not a leader. He did not like school and was not a good student. At about the age of nine, his father had a streak of bad business luck and the Marshalls financial situation made it necessary for young George to leave Miss Thompson's School and enroll in the public school. There it was discovered he couldn't read well and knew hardly anything about mathematics. George was embarrassed, and his father was horrified by his lack of knowledge compared to other children of his age. George seemed to be a slow learner, was not an able student, and his teachers thought he couldn't learn.

Being tall for his age, with large feet and rather shy, as well as not seeming very smart, caused other students to make fun of him. Being laughed at made school even worse.

"I had a very painful time in the public school because I was ashamed to admit my ignorance and so many in the room knew these . . . (math) problems---so quickly and so much better than I did . . . If it was history, that was all right; I could star in history. But the other things I was very, very poor in. . ."

One bright side to being in the public school was a, ". . . pretty girl I was devoted to though she didn't pay any attention to me."

He liked her enough to try to learn to spell, so that he could stand beside her at the head of the line in the spelling bee. And he made it there one day, but missed the next word and had to go back to the end of the line. He said that his "love had its limits" and he "never tried again."

George liked to succeed at whatever he did, and to avoid above all else, complete failure. He didn't like to do what he couldn't do well. He never liked spelling and he hated to be last.

When he was fourteen his father learned from the school principal that George was not doing well, and he was so annoyed with George that he didn't speak to him for three days.

"I did not like school. The truth is I was not even a poor student, I simply was not a student and my academic record was a sad affair. . . . I never learnt how to study until. . . I went away to school."

From the public school, George was entered at Professor Hopkins' Academy on the second floor of the Tetlow Hotel. He wasn't a good student there, either. That wasn't much of a school, anyway, and it closed shortly after George enrolled.

The public high school, Central School, in Uniontown may have been where he graduated. Regardless of which school he attended, George C. Marshall was not well prepared for college. Thank goodness he was an independent learner, liked reading of all kinds, learned well from other sources, and had several good summers for growing.

Chapter 6

Ready . . . Set . . . Go!

Growing boys need a lot of exercise and George was certainly growing. As a brand new teenager, his height began to match the size of his feet! He tried his best to succeed in sports, but his talents were limited.

The competition and the planning it took to play football made it interesting to him and for awhile he played on the private school's team. However, he was too lightweight and too skinny. And he hurt his arm.

Somehow, while playing football probably, he injured his elbow and it stayed injured for life. There were no x-rays at that time, so it was impossible for a doctor to "see the problem." They just had to guess at it. George could feel it! The tendons were the problem.

" . . . the tendons had been pulled and gotten out of the main joint. . . . "

A knot formed on his elbow as the body grew more bone around the tendons and made the arm very sensitive to any touch. And that finished off football for a time.

Baseball was almost impossible because he couldn't throw. He had to bowl instead of pitch. He couldn't bat, at least not well, for he didn't have enough strength in the arm to have a forceful batting swing. His right elbow just wouldn't let him.

The position he often played, when he did play, was catcher. Whenever he showed up for games, and the choosing of the sides began, he was almost always picked last----last again.

Not being able to play sports well didn't keep him from being interested. He wasn't quite twelve in September of 1892 when he ran to meet the 8:15 train to bring home the newspaper. George and his parents were keen to read the account of the boxing match between John L. Sullivan and James J. Corbett. It was the first professional fight that was fought using padded boxing gloves! Corbett won.

Another time, when Corbett lost to Fitzsimmons, George and his friends stood outside the telegraph office window to hear the fight reports read as they came in over the wire. Radio was not available when George Marshall was a boy!

Sledding was a popular sport in the winter. George Marshall had great fun at that, even with the risk of making his bad arm worse.

When the snow got packed into perfect condition on the street, someone would be posted on watch at Main Street to stop traffic for a sled that was coming through, right across town. They surely couldn't stop the sled!

"They had these big sleds they called 'Panics', . . . where the head man sat with a skate on one foot, his legs crossed over, and guided the sled (holding) on with two hands. . ."

George had a Flexible Flyer, one of the best kind to have, and one of the few in town. He and his buddies added a plank on top of it to extend the length so that two more people could ride. He liked it most when his father and his father's friends went along.

"On a moonlight night, . . . I sat in front with the skate on my foot . . .and my father would. . . . sit behind and was supposed to swing the sled . . .and we would come down this road. It had walks across the road which . . . really made 'jumpers' as we called them, and the sled would leap out from (the jumpers) and you had to be very expert to sit and prevent it turning turtle when it landed on the other side of the crossing.

"The whole town would turn out, and it was quite a fine sport to have all the men, old and young, and the boys all playing together. And playing together was what it was."

But life wasn't all fun and games for the teenage George and his friends. They lived in an era of rapid changes. History books refer to the years between 1880 and 1910 as the Industrial Revolution. Inventions and improvements were made every day in the work world and in the home world. As time ran out for the nineteenth century, so did the old ways of doing and making things. The 1890's was a time of adventure.

When the first telephones came to Uniontown, George Marshall was among the first in town to talk to somebody in Chicago. The world was growing up and so was the boy, by George!

CHAPTER 7
BICYCLES, WATERMELONS AND CHICKEN FIGHTING

When George C. Marshall was growing up, summertime in Pennsylvania, for boys, meant being outside, going places and doing things. As teen-agers, George and Andy had lots of energy and Andy's grandfather had a farm. The boys went there to help with the haying or the threshing of the wheat. They worked hard and ate their meals with the farmhands.

Work started at daybreak and went until sunset. Twelve o'clock dinner was large and prepared by Andy's grandmother and her helpers. All teenagers like to eat!

"We played a great deal in the country . . .Andy's grandfather had this very valuable farm which they farmed in the splendid way of those days . . . when we could go out there, we would be allowed to sit at the table with the harvest hands. . . The conversation at the table seems to me smacked very much of that I get in Westerns.

I read of the cowboys in the West, where they are always making fun of each other and dressing down one of their members, if he in any way seemed to brag . . . but I never heard of any fighting . . . I helped out in the field hauling in the hay shocks. . . I helped in distributing the manure. . . I learned a great deal about it without being conscious I was learning. . . .When we got bicycles, . . . we could go there much more frequently. We were always rewarded with whole pies, and that was a wonderful thing."

Bicycles came into common use around 1894 allowing George and his friends to travel on their own, anywhere they chose. Well, at least as far as another town.

"I first rode . . .the tall bicycle with the little wheel behind and most of the time I was on my nose. Then came the 'safety,' as they called it which had spade-like handles and a hard rubber tire and was a very heavy machine. Then . . .the inflated tire and the light machine.

"I learnt to be very expert in changing the tire because we had lots of punctures. . .I picked up things that seemed very distant and very remote. . . until I got into the bicycle. . . Brownsville was remote from me. It was only twelve miles but (we) practically never saw it until we got bicycles."

Sometimes, in the summer, he also got a job.

"They built up at home the first ice plant in that part of the country, and I became a temporary employee of the ice plant whenever I could get the job and have the time in the summer."

His father bought big watermelons on Saturdays, and on Sundays George put them in the ice house among the blocks of ice. On Sunday afternoon, after church and the big Sunday dinner were finished, the town boys came to the Marshalls' yard. George went for the watermelons with his wagon and Mr. Marshall cut them into large V-like pieces. That was the Sunday afternoon entertainment. Eating watermelon and spitting seeds.

"As I recall, the melons cost about ten cents apiece."

Another job for George was assisting an engineer who was working on the national geological survey and the making of maps of the Uniontown area. George held the stadia rod while the engineer did the measuring. George's job was important, but tiresome and boring, and his attention wandered at times. One day George was not holding the rod correctly, and the engineer became irritated.

"I sought an excuse, as a boy always does, and I told him I was looking at that bird on the fence, which as I recall was a swallow. . ."

The engineer angrily asked what was so special about the bird.

"And without any real idea of what was happening or why I was doing it . . . I walked over to the fence and picked up this swallow. It wasn't wounded; he didn't fly and I picked him up."

The engineer was speechless. He thought George had some secret and special ability to handle birds, that he was a wizard or something magical.

"And then I turned him loose and he flew off.. . .But I never had a similar occurrence in my life. But it dug me out of that embarrassment of being rather asleep on the job."

That was an unexpected bird adventure, but George and Andy became involved in another type of bird adventure--- quite a bit of fowl play!

In those days of the mid 1890s, men gathered in barns or around a shallow pit located in isolated country areas and bet money on chicken fights. Roosters were fitted out with spurs (sharpened nails wrapped around their legs), paired off according to size, and thrown into a pit to fight until one rooster killed the other.

That was nothing new, but when George and Andy got involved, it was adventure for them. They had raised chickens for a year or so. They first raised bantams which are small sized chickens.

Once they invited George's mother out to see the bantam roosters, because his mother asked why he spent so much time in the chicken house. He and Andy showed her how the little roosters would fight and the Bantams seemed to her to be more cute and funny than dangerous. Mrs. Marshall figured they were only innocent pets.

Little did Mrs. Marshall know! When she left, they put the nails onto the feet of the bantams and then those little birds were quite dangerous, to each other.   Also, the boys had ordered some eggs from Georgia and were raising Georgia Reds, which are large sized chickens. And they trained those roosters to really fight!

Boys couldn't enter the "main," or fighting contests, so their blacksmith friend, George Gadd, did it for them. He was their "performer," or trainer, and he"pitted," their roosters, got them ready and into the pits to fight.

George C, Marshall loved animals of all kinds and, even though a bird usually ended up dead, he enjoyed watching the cockfights. It was a little like war. Perhaps he enjoyed the adventure of it all---slipping away to a secret place, knowing the passwords and handshakes of the performers who carried their prize roosters in wicker baskets---being sneaky and illegal.

On one of the fight days, the boys went to watch. They drove a horse and cart far out into the country and into a thicket of trees, tied the horse in a safe place, and walked to the fighting area. George Gadd would be 'pitting' their roosters.

Men from as far away as Pittsburgh had brought their best fighters and there was a crowd of forty to fifty men placing their bets on the 'spats,' or fights. George and Andy stayed on the edge of the crowd of rowdy gamblers. They knew they shouldn't be there.

"There were forty or fifty men and . . . very heavy betting . . . the affair had just gotten underway when we were raided and most of these men were herded in. . . . Andy and myself were experts in rapid motion under such circumstances."

47

They ran! They hid in the woods all afternoon to avoid being caught. When all was quiet, they started looking for each other. Creeping as quietly as an Indian, George knew someone else was in the woods, but he wasn't sure who. After a few hours, the two boys discovered they were tracking each other!

But where was the horse and cart? They were afraid someone had made off with them both, or maybe it had been taken by the sheriff's men as evidence! They would be caught for sure.

Luckily the boys only had their directions confused and needed to turn back. They finally found the horse where they had left it, still grazing happily. They arrived home at one o'clock in the morning after being gone since early the morning before.

Once again, George's mother protected him by letting him tell her, and not his father, where he had been and what he had done.

She didn't have to scold him. He had learned a lesson. That type of lesson George Marshall learned quickly. He didn't have to study it for hours at a time. For the studying kind of lessons, George C. Marshall had to go to college.

CHAPTER 8

A RAT IN ROOM 88

When George C. Marshall was about ten years old, his brother Stuart went away to the Virginia Military Institute in Lexington, Virginia "and came back all military." So at the end of his Uniontown schooling, George told his parents that he wanted to attend the institute, also. They were doubtful. Stuart was alarmed!

"When I was begging to go to VMI, I overheard Stuart talking to my mother; he was trying to persuade her not to let me go because he thought I would disgrace the family name. ...Well, that made more impression on me than all instructors, parental pressure, or anything else. I decided right then I was going to wipe his eye."

He'd show Stuart a thing or two!

In the late eighteen hundreds, if a boy was serious about a military career, he went to West Point. George Marshall was such a poor student he couldn't have passed West Point's required entrance examination.

His injured arm might have prevented his passing the physical examination for West Point. Also, to go to West Point a boy had to be appointed, and his appointment depended on his father's political status.

A senator or a congressmen recommended a boy for appointment to West Point and, at that time, Pennsylvania's congressmen were Republicans while Mr. Marshall was a staunch Democrat, so politics was not on George's side. He didn't apply to West Point.

There is no record of any academic examination given to George for entrance to VMI. Politics didn't count, he had a strong Virginia name, there were seven other Marshalls at VMI, his father was known there, and his brother had graduated from there. That was all it took to get him in. That, plus some money his mother had from the sale of some land she owned.

George's parents did not encourage him to enter a military career. They didn't think he would have a successful future if he became a soldier. There was no social status, no assured success or advancement, and it certainly didn't pay much money.

But George was determined to go to VMI, and go he did. He went by train.

Train travel was fairly quick and reliable by that time of the century, much better than stage coaches. The trains going into Lexington had to climb a steep hill, so they turned around below town and backed up the hill to the station. As the train left Lexington, it was easier for the engineer to go forward rather than backwards.

Lexington, in Virginia's Shenandoah Valley between Roanoke and Harrisonburg, was named in 1778 and is the county seat of Rockbridge County.

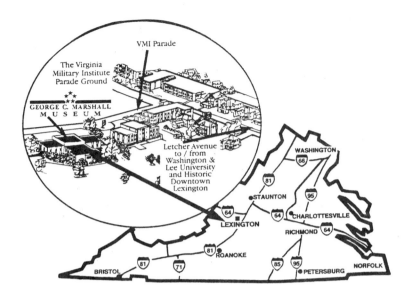

The Virginia Military Institute Parade Ground

VMI Parade

GEORGE C. MARSHALL MUSEUM

Letcher Avenue to / from Washington & Lee University and Historic Downtown Lexington

WASHINGTON 66

STAUNTON 81 95

64 LEXINGTON 64 CHARLOTTESVILLE

RICHMOND 64

81 ROANOKE

BRISTOL 81 77

85 95 PETERSBURG NORFOLK

In 1897, about 3,200 people lived in the town. The streets were dirt-and-gravel and the business section small. Courthouse business and the markets brought people into town from all around the county.

Stonewall Jackson and Robert E. Lee were buried there, so Lexington was popular with tourists interested in the Civil War. A hundred years later, it still is.

The main business in Lexington was, and still is, education. Two colleges were born and grew up near the town. One is Virginia Military Institute, a state-supported military four-year college, and the other is Washington and Lee University, a privately-supported four-year college and law school, named for George Washington and Robert E. Lee.

In 1897, both schools stood on a ridge above the main streets of town, standing side by side, their campus grounds touching. A hundred years later, they still do.

Today Virginia Military Institute is a four-year, state-supported military college with about thirteen hundred students. Until 1997, it was traditionally an all male school, and proud of it.

As a college, VMI had a rather strange beginning. After the War of 1812, Virginia had several arsenals around the state, storing left-over ammunition and guns and the Lexington Arsenal was one of them. The twenty-five young men guarding the arsenal tended to be loud and rowdy, which concerned some of the town's people. They wanted somebody to do something about those boys and their noise.

A local lawyer, J.T.L. Preston, proposed the arsenal be turned into a military school for young men and, so, with financial help from the state of Virginia, it was. In November of 1839, twenty-eight cadets, following strict military rules, made up the first student body of the Virginia Military Institute. Rules became tradition and tradition ruled the school.

The enrollment in 1897 of 221 cadets, ranging in age from 16 to 21, was the largest since 1875 and included a freshman class of 122.

VMI began its school year on the first day of September. George Marshall arrived in Lexington on September 11, 1897. He was late, and he was last. . . again. His delayed arrival was caused by typhoid fever, a common disease of the times, that he had caught from swimming in a pond.

George's father sent a letter along with him to the president of the school, Superintendent Scott Shipp, that read, "I send you my youngest, and last. He is bright, full of life, and I believe will get along very well." He included a check for $200 for the first semester's tuition, room and meals, and uniforms. The year's cost for out of state students then was three hundred and sixty-five dollars.

As George Marshall walked from the train station, he crossed the W&L campus passing by the Lee Chapel and onto the VMI post through the Limit Gates. There, at the edge of the parade ground, he stopped to watch the scene before him. Evening Parade was about to begin. He said, some sixty years later,

"I will never forget walking down the long approach avenue to barracks and hearing the bugle sound the assembly for dress parade and seeing the adjutant and the sergeant major strut out to form the line on which the battalion would form. They were very wonderful looking figures to me."

Suddenly, excited and happy, the ordinary boy from Uniontown knew he wanted to become a part of that scene. At the age of sixteen, he was going to become a VMI cadet!

Every cadet begins VMI life at the end of the line--- last---as a freshman, a fourth classman---known as 'the lowest form of student life'---a Rat. George Marshall probably learned in about five minutes that VMI life and language was different from any other in the outside world.

He also learned that the VMI class system is like this: freshmen are Rats or Fourth Classmen, sophomores are Third Classmen, juniors are Second Classmen, and seniors are First Classmen. All of these get shortened to Firsts, Seconds, Thirds, and Rats.

54

In the barracks, the different levels or floors, are called 'Stoops'. Today the Firsts live on the First Stoop (the first floor) and the Seconds on the Second Stoop, and so on. In 1897, there weren't as many students, or as many rooms in the barracks.

The classrooms and administration offices were on the First Stoop. The Seconds and Firsts were on the Second Stoop, Thirds were on the Third Stoop, and the Fourths on the Fourth Stoop. Since he was the last of his class to arrive, he was assigned to the last available room space for Rats. But the room wasn't where it should have been.

With so many freshmen, there was no more room on the Fourth. He found three roommates, waiting for him in Room 88, on the Third Stoop! On the Third Stoop? Living with the Thirds? Oh, poor George C. Marshall!

Their room was about twenty-one by seventeen feet in size and contained a wooden table for study, wire and mattress cots, straight chairs, a wardrobe, slop jars and a washstand (instead of a bathroom). Its one window and the bare walls made it look a bit like a prison cell. About the only convenience in the barracks was electricity, which had arrived in 1893.

Water had to be carried in buckets from an outside spigot. They poured the water into their basins for washing hands and faces. Sometimes in the winter, the room was so cold the water froze in the basin during the night.

Since there was no running water inside the barracks, the toilets were outside, too, of course! The installing of inside bathrooms was one of the best things to happen in George's first year at VMI.

55

A steam-type of central heating system in the barracks had been installed in 1850, when Stonewall Jackson was a teacher there. It provided some heat. Little good it did Rats!

Rats were required to sleep with their windows open. George strapped his blanket across his bed to keep out the cold air. Sometimes he found snow on his bed in the mornings!

George and his roommates were the only Rats to live on the Third Stoop. That put them in perfect range for being teased, taunted and tormented, being put through the initiation ritual known as hazing.

Hazing was not approved of by the school officials or administration, but they knew it happened. Cadets could be expelled for hazing, if or when they were caught. Still, it was a favorite sport of the Third Classmen. The risk of being caught made their 'duty' more exciting!

It was acceptable for Third Classmen to boss the Rats around and aggravate them, that wasn't bad hazing. When ordered to, "Fin Out!" a Rat stood at exaggerated attention with his stomach sucked in, chest thrust out, chin pulled in and held down to his chest, and arms squeezed to his sides, with palms facing forward. He could be ordered to recite rules, answer silly questions, be called 'the lowest form of life' or worse, and just get yelled at for the fun of it.

Rats had to do chores, run errands, do push-ups, anything a Third told them to do whether it made any sense or not. One of George's first roommates left after two months.

"Fin Out Rat" 1900 Style

56

One favorite trick in hazing was called 'chicken fighting', and it wasn't the kind George Marshall knew of in Uniontown. In VMI chicken fights, a bed was unrolled, the Rat stretched out across it and the bed was rolled up and strapped around him. Only his head and feet were left out free.

Two Rats were 'pitted' against each other! They had to buck and bump each other until one fell down leaving the winner standing. Rats had to be careful about how they fell, if they could, so as not to hit their heads on the tables or hard floor.

George C. Marshall was tall, lanky, awkward and shy. Third Classmen made life miserable for Rats like George with hazing. They went after Marshall because of his lack of military skill, his quiet manner, and his Yankee accent.

He wasn't any good at drill or marching, but the Thirds found that he could certainly sweat, look miserable and turn red-faced if spoken to or corrected. That made it even more fun to tease him.

One night, not long after his arrival, George was given a 'test of endurance' of another sort. He was ordered to squat over a bayonet, sharp point up, until he was told to stand. The bout with typhoid fever had left him weak and easily tired. His endurance didn't last long, only twenty minutes. He slipped!

The bayonet gashed his buttock giving him a close call with a serious injury. He went to the infirmary doctor who treated him, and George Marshall missed drill for four days, but he did not report to any authority what had happened. In other words, he didn't tell!

The Thirds were probably glad about that, because they were not caught and sent home. George wasn't bothered much with hazing after that.

"It was part of the business and the only thing to do was to accept it as best you could."

The daily routine of a cadet, new or old, was not much fun. The getting-up bugle (reveille) was heard at 6:20 a.m. with roll call five minutes later and breakfast at seven. Their room had to be cleaned and ready for inspection by eight. Any visible dust, dirt or disorder---and a cadet deserved demerits! Every five demerits meant an hour of penalty tour---walking and carrying a pack and/or a rifle.

Every morning four hours of classes came before lunch and then more classes until four p.m. followed by military drill until five. Fifteen minutes was allowed to get into their dress uniform and ready for evening parade!

Following Evening Parade, the cadets had supper and after supper, they had half an hour of free time before they started the 7-10 study period. Then, lights out. With a day like that, they probably had no trouble going to sleep.

Starting in September, the school year lasted until the end of June, with only a few one-day holidays and no long Christmas vacation. There were classes on Saturday until one o'clock. Then, if he didn't have to walk 'penalty tours' to work off demerits, a cadet was allowed two hours in town.

On Sundays, all cadets marched to church and after lunch they could go out in the country, but not to town, as long as they were back for evening parade. All cadets marched to meals and to classes and again at Evening Parade.

According to the Book of Orders, 'Silence and soldier-like deportment shall be required of all cadets while on class parade and while marching to the recitation rooms or place of instruction.'

Within the first few days of arriving, Marshall met up with another VMI tradition called "growlie" in the mess hall. It was a hash-like mush of leftovers from one dinner all thrown together for the next dinner! Upper classmen did not allow Rats to have peaceful meals or long ones. That was good, especially when the meal was "growlie."

According to General Marshall, "The mess was a pretty stern affair."

Two events marked Marshall's Rat year as different from any other. In October, the VMI cadet corps was invited and went to Nashville for the Tennessee Centennial Exposition. Each cadet had to pay $7 for the trip which lasted a week. They went by train, stopping in Louisville, Kentucky on the way home to give a parade.

The second event occurred six months later, in April of 1898, when the Spanish- American War offered the U.S. a chance to become involved in world affairs. As soon as war was declared, the VMI corps of cadets voted to volunteer "their services to their government to fight for their country."

The cadets' help was not accepted. Volunteers of U.S. National Guard units did the country's fighting in that short war. Among the units sent to the Philippine Islands was the 10th Pennsylvania Regiment, which included Company C from Uniontown. Also, 136 former VMI men were in the Spanish-American War and the Phillippines conflict. George Marshall was keenly interested in the reports of battles and injuries, for he knew many of the men. He followed the war closely by way of the newspaper.

Even as a new war began, on May 15 of 1898 the VMI cadets remembered that other war from thirty-three years earlier, the Civil War.

On May 11, 1864, the entire VMI corps formed ranks in front of the barracks. Some were left on guard duty, but Lt. Col. Scott Shipp (Superintendent) led 241 cadets as they marched to New Market, eighty miles away, in four days.

They went to reinforce the 62nd Virginia Regiment of the Confederate Army as they met Union forces. This is the only time the entire student body of an American college has fought as a unit in a war.

On May 15, 1864, ten cadets were killed, and many were wounded. Six of the dead were buried at VMI. Every year the Battle of New Market is remembered with special ceremonies and the six graves are decorated with wreaths.

When George C. Marshall first observed New Market Day, there was a parade in the morning and a full dress parade in the evening. At both times, the corps lined up as it would have in 1864, marching into place to the slow beat of a drum. Mrs. Stonewall Jackson came to watch the New Market ceremonies, too, the year that George C. Marshall was a Rat.

During the day, at every formation, the roll call of the dead was made, and as each name was called out, an appointed cadet answered, "Killed on the field of honor, sir." At the evening parade, a twenty-one gun salute was fired and Taps were sounded. The corps then marched slowly and silently back to barracks.

This ceremony never failed to impress Marshall. His great uncle had been a cadet in the battle at New Market. The New Market Day ceremony was a tradition then. It still is.

George was so interested in the Battle of New Market that he learned all about it, why and how it happened and exactly where it was fought. He had maps and would spread them out on the study table and lecture his roommates (or any cadet that would listen) about the strategies and the problems of the battle. No other Rat knew more than he did about the Battle of New Market.

Between September and June, Marshall worked hard to become a good cadet. He learned how to drill, how to wear a uniform, and how to march. He learned about self-control, discipline and leadership. He concentrated on being military because he was 'running for corp', the highest military rank in his class.

At the end of the school year, he was appointed First Corporal of Cadets for the next year. And he didn't fail any of his classes! He placed above the middle in his class academically. And he had earned zero demerits!

". . . The first year was quite an ordeal, though I came afterwards, like all the rest of my friends, to look back on it with more appreciation than I did any other year."

He went home for the summer of 1898 to Uniontown looking proud in his VMI uniform, showing off the corporal's stripe on his sleeve, walking taller and straighter, looking healthier and heavier. He was downright pleased with himself!

When his picture was taken at home, he pushed his arm forward so the corporal's stripe could be easily seen.

George C. Marshall had survived, quite successfully, being a Rat in room 88. He wasn't just an ordinary Uniontown boy anymore, he was a VMI cadet.

A possible train route for Cadet Marshall.

Chesapeake and Ohio Railway

" THE RHINE, THE ALPS, AND THE BATTLEFIELD LINE."

TWO MODEL TRAINS

BETWEEN

NEW YORK	PHILADELPHIA	BALTIMORE
WASHINGTON	OLD POINT	RICHMOND
	LEXINGTON, VA.	
CINCINNATI	LOUISVILLE	INDIANAPOLIS
ST. LOUIS	CHICAGO	SOUTH and WEST

H. W. FULLER, General Passenger Agent,

WASHINGTON, D. C.

64

CHAPTER 9

TEN-SHUN!

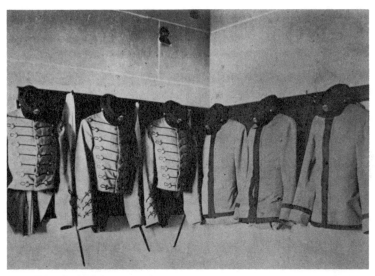

The Spanish-American War was over in August of 1898, and September found George C. Marshall back at the Virginia Military Institute for his second year.

Most cadets are given nicknames in their Rat year. In Uniontown, George had been called Flicker, because of the color of his hair. At VMI, he was nicknamed Pug because of the shape of his nose. Somebody, making fun of his Pittsburgh twang and the manner in which he pronounced the letter R, slipped an R into Pug and, to some cadets, Pug became Purg!

His one returning roommate, Leonard Nicholson, was simply called Nick. They lived in room 73 on the Third Stoop with a new roommate, Philip B. (Buster) Peyton. The three got along well together, became good friends and were roommates for the next three years.

As Thirds, this was their year to pester the Rats, getting revenge for all they had suffered the year before. But some Thirds were really too keen on hazing.

During the 1898-99 year, a severe hazing spree got several cadets dismissed from school. The ring leader of the hazers and some others were disciplined. General Scott Shipp sent them home---expelled them.

The Thirds, as a class, were so indignant to this treatment of their classmates that, with very few exceptions, the entire class resigned from VMI. General Shipp, or "Old Billy" (he had a goatee and so do billy goats), called a Third Stoop meeting, and expressed his opinion (which wasn't a good one) of the "mutiny." He put his watch on the table and gave them five minutes to withdraw their resignations or else, "proceed to your homes."

The Thirds were mad and stubborn. They took the full time to give in, and for a few minutes it appeared that the railroad would have a big business day--- taking them all away from Lexington. Finally, they surrendered. They weren't happy, but they stayed.

Thirds considered hazing to be their duty and usually did it well. Nick and Buster probably did their share of hazing, but George had larger responsibilities.

Being one of the tallest cadets, at almost six feet, he certainly stood out among them. His sharp voice was easily recognized as he barked out the military commands, and it was said that he could be heard the length of the parade ground! He wore his "grays" with a white waist belt and white gloves and carried a ramrod (a stick used for putting powder into the muzzle of a gun) in practice. Whenever in formation and in command, he was strictly military.

As First Corporal in Company A, he was responsible for the squad of cadets. He saw to it that his cadets were where they were supposed to be in formation. When the count was made, if any of his squad was found missing, Marshall found out where they were and why, making sure all was well. The First Corporal reported to the First Sergeant if cadets were missing, and the reason for the absence..

The First Corporal also had to take his turn as Corporal of the Guard. When being Corporal of the Guard, Marshall carried a set of keys on his bayonet scabbard, stayed in the Officer of the Day's office, and helped the O.D. with whatever needed to be done. The Officer of the Day was largely responsible for the general discipline of the barracks.

It was the O.D.'s duty to sock (report) any cadets he saw violating regulations and the O.D. held the corporals of the guard responsible for any violations he saw. If the guard didn't make a report and the O.D. knew it, the guard got socked also.

George C. Marshall socked all violators he saw---old cadets, Rats, his own classmates---it didn't matter who they were. But he didn't go out of his way to find somebody to sock, and he never made any enemies or lost any friends in the performance of his duties, because he was always fair.

67

Marshall was highly respected by his classmates and, when off duty he was just Pug Marshall---a likeable, boyish, and happy fellow.

Henry Peck Fry from Tennessee, was one of several cadets that transferred into VMI as Thirds in 1898. Fry was impressed with George C. Marshall's military style and ability as well as his personality.

Fry kept a journal and he wrote, "Room 73 was the Mecca of the Thirds and during recreation hours was always full of visitors. Marshall and Co. were excellent hosts. Although military on the outside, Purg in his room, was a lazy-looking, good natured person. . . fond of listening to good stories and telling them. . .

"He always joined us in our songs and yells and, while as a 'songbird' he was an excellent corporal, he got a lot of kick out singing and yelling and made his share of the noise."

From the start of the year, Marshall was a "running corp" according to Fry, which meant he was running (trying) for sergeant! In the Third Class picture which appeared in the year book, The Bomb, George Marshall's arm is draped across the shoulder of the cadet in front of him, so everyone can see his stripes, again. Just in case they missed seeing them before.

In his second year at V.M.I., George had to work hard at his studies, as well as being an officer. Thirds had to follow a set course of study taking Mathematics (which he never learned to like), French, English (which he disliked) and History (which he loved) Astronomy, Physics and Drawing. As always he struggled with his studies to make passing grades.

The Thirds had their adventures at misbehaving, but that wasn't unexpected. In fact, their behavior was traditional, and tradition was important at VMI.

One favorite tradition was painting Old George--- painting the life-size bronze statute of George Washington that stood outside the barracks archway. For weeks, certain Thirds collected brushes and paint and stashed them safely away.

The job had to be done late at night while everyone was asleep, except for the Third that was on guard duty, walking back and forth in front of the statue, and the chosen few who would do the painting. Nobody else knew exactly when the deed would be done.

When everything was ready, the Corporal of the Guard gave the signal and the guard on duty turned his back so that he could truthfully say later he "didn't see who did the painting." The next morning, to everyone's surprise, there stood Old George, straight and solid as ever, and beautiful in the Third Class colors of purple and white!

Colors can be considered to be a custom or tradition. Countries, classes, and colleges use specific colors for flags, emblems, clothes, and a variety of decorations. Just as our country uses red, white and blue in its flag, VMI uses red, white, and yellow for theirs. These colors were adopted by the school officials in 1900 and at that time represented the different military divisions -- the artillery, the infantry, and the cavalry. They are a vital part of the school's traditions and are still in use today.

The George Washington statue - 1900

Another custom that perhaps George C. Marshall took part in was known as "taking in the Rats." Each Rat bent over a study table and several Thirds lined up and took one turn at swatting the Rat's behind with a flexible leather bayonet scabbard with a brass tipped end. After each swat, the Rat stood up and shook hands with the Third who had hit him, was called by his last name or given a nickname, and welcomed as a classmate. Rats didn't really belong at VMI, not until they had been "taken in."

George Marshall made it through his second year at VMI without any demerits and, when the cadet officer promotions were announced, there was celebrating in room 73 on the Third stoop. Congratulating George Marshall on well-deserved success was getting to be a habit for his classmates.

Once more, George Marshall went home to Uniontown in June and, once more he could claim fine military success and medium academic success. He stood twenty-fifth out of sixty-nine academically, and another stripe was added to his uniform sleeve. George C. Marshall had attained the position of First Sergeant. Big responsibilities were ahead of him at VMI, but first came the summer and an incident that would seal his fate.

CHAPTER 10
LEADER OF THE LINE

In August of 1899, George C. Marshall was in Uniontown when the Uniontown Company of the 10th Pennsylvania Volunteer Infantry returned home from the Philippines. Uniontown gave them a hero's welcome complete with a parade along Main Street, where the bricks that paved the street had been painted red, white and blue. George C. Marshall watched the parade, and the parade had a significant impact on his future.

"I have sometimes thought that the impressions of that period, and particularly of that parade, had a determining effect on my choice of a profession . . . . It was a grand American small town demonstration of pride in its young men and of wholesome enthusiasm over their achievements. Years later most of us realized it was much more than that. It reflected the introduction of America into the affairs of the world beyond the seas."

When he returned to Lexington and VMI for his third year in September of 1899, George and his roommates, Buster and Nick, lived in Room 34 on the Second Stoop. George was the First Sergeant of Company "A"and very keen to be a soldier in the real army. Seconds didn't have to bother with hazing and could concentrate on military classes and their studies.

This was the year to decide on his curriculum major. At that time, VMI students could choose between electrical engineering, civil engineering or chemistry, and he chose civil engineering.

He had a great interest in surveying and map making and considerable aptitude for both. He knew he certainly had more ability in engineering than in chemistry, English, or math!

As First Sergeant, he assumed heavy responsibilities and thrived on them. He memorized the company roll call, and he called the roll seven times a day, six days a week and twice on Sunday!

The First Sergeant kept the company roster, the morning report and the sick report. He received reports from the other first sergeants and had disciplinary and sick reports to write each night. Because of his reports, Marshall could keep his light on in his room until 10:30, half an hour after Taps. This was lucky for Nick and Buster. They could study for a half hour longer!

Henry Fry wrote about Marshall, "In his 2nd Class year, his tension disappeared. The difference in his way of living and acting immediately showed itself... He had always been pleasant and likeable, but now he was more relaxed and at ease, more affable and mellow."

Marshall was almost certain to be named First Captain, the highest military rank a cadet can attain. Yet he was careful not to slip up and or let down in his "running." Inattention to duty was not Marshall's way. He kept a close eye on the discipline and the military appearance of his company.

When he had been a Rat and a private in the rear rank of Company A, the First Sergeant had barked at him, "Fin Out, Mr. Marshall!" Now it was his turn to yell, "Fin Out!", to manage and control both new and old cadets, and he did a good job of it.

His uniform had white cross belts with a brass breast plate, a straight sword with scabbard on a leather belt, a red silk sash around his waist and white gloves and he carried a rifle. He was faithful in his duty, day in and day out without variation. While Marshall was its top sergeant, "A" Company was the smartest looking and the best disciplined company in the corps.

He worked hard at his military duty and on his academics, but all work and no play was no fun, either. In September, a circus came to East Lexington. Purg Marshall went along with his classmates on a Saturday afternoon to take in the sights and activities, one of which he should have left alone.

A man was taking bets on a "shell game". Three walnut shells were on a flat surface and a pea was put under one shell. The man moved the shells around quickly and completely, then asked them to guess where the pea was. If you bet $1 and won, he would pay you another dollar, but if you missed, you lost your dollar.

The boys were interested. George Marshall was sure he knew how the trick worked. One cadet, who could afford it, bet and lost. George had a monthly allowance of five dollars. It was early in the month, so he bet his $5, feeling sure he would go away with ten. Sadly enough, he lost. That was probably his last encounter with carnival games.

On their way home, they sat on the front steps of a house for a group picture taken by a traveling photographer. George was probably upset about losing his allowance. It was a warm afternoon, and so his collar was unbuttoned. This is the only picture of Marshall in non-correct uniform, being "grossly unmilitary."

During his first two years, he had kept a promise to his mother not to play football. She was afraid he would damage his already injured arm even more, but once he was a Second, he was free of the promise, and he went out for the football team. He became a substitute and started to show some promise as a player. VMI defeated W & L by a score of 39-0! The season ended with only one game played.

VMI closed for a six-week furlough in mid-October due to an epidemic of Typhoid Fever. Unsanitary conditions had to be corrected, and more modern plumbing and toilets installed before school began again on November 28th. To make up for lost time, the cadets had to go through much longer class sessions and longer study hours. That school year didn't end until July.

At the end of his third year, George C. Marshall once again had no demerits. He ranked first in military again and again about the middle of his class in academics. Out of 42 Second Classmen, he was 19th. His best subject of the year was U.S. Drill Regulations!

Graduation Day on July 4th brought along the announcements of the promotions and appointments for the next year. Of the twenty-one sergeants in the "running" only four could become a company captain because there were only four companies. Only one could be First Captain. George C. Marshall was announced as the First Captain putting him in charge of the entire corps of cadets.

Henry Fry wrote, ". . . he had reached the pinnacle of success at VMI. Wearing his new captain's chevrons and wrapped in a red sash, sword, and plume, Marshall went on duty as the Officer of the Day for his first time."

An Officer of the Day can see as much or as little as he wants to see, depending on whether or not he wants to see it. An O.D. can be most disagreeable! As Officer of the Day, George Marshall reported anything he saw that was wrong, but didn't go out of his way to find trouble. VMI operated on an honor code system. A cadet did not lie, cheat or steal or tolerate one who did. It's the same today.

At that time a formal dance, the Final Ball, was held on the night of Graduation Day. It was a tradition for the Seconds to give the Ball for the seniors. The Final Ball of 1900 was quite an eleborate affair.

The gymnasium of Jackson Hall was decorated beautifully, dance music was provided by a band, and plenty of pretty "calics" (girls) dressed in white and carrying armsful of long-stemmed, red, American Beauty roses were there.

Officers of the Final Ball were elected to do the planning of the Ball. They also had the honor of leading the Grand March that began the evening's dancing. George C. Marshall was Vice-President, so he and his date were second in line as the officers walked onto the floor.

Kate Fauntleroy from Staunton, Virginia was his partner for the opening dance, but she was not his "calic." (Calic came from the word calico which is a type of dress material, and girls wear dresses, so at VMI a 'calic" was a girlfriend.) Kate was just an acquaintance of George Marshall and a necessary companion for the dance.

In June of 1900, a busy time in his life, George C. Marshall was not much interested in romance and wasn't singing love songs. However, he changed his tune on that subject a few months later.

The pleasure of your presence is requested

at the

Final Ball

Wednesday July fourth at ten o'clock.

Patronesses

Mrs. Hoge Tyler	Va.	Mrs. A. N. Reade	Va.
Mrs. Fitzhugh Lee	Cuba.	Mrs. H. C. Ford	Va.
Mrs. W. L. Kelly	Va.	Mrs. R. A. Marr	Va.
Mrs. G. C. Marshall	Pa.	Mrs. T. M. Semmes	Va.
Mrs. T. T. Hubard	Va.	Mrs. L. B. Walker	Va.
Mrs. Edward Echols	Va.	Mrs. Morgan Pendleton	Va.
Mrs. H. C. Hudgins	Va.	Mrs. Francis Mallory	Va.
Mrs. Hunter Pendleton	Va.	Mrs. T. P. Grasty	Ky.
Mrs. G. D. Breeler	Tex.	Mrs. T. H. Brokenborough	Va.
Mrs. N. B. Tucker	Va.	Miss M. W. Freeland	Va.
Mrs. C. S. Roller	Va.	Mrs. J. M. Miller	Va.

CHAPTER 11

LAST, BUT NOT LEAST

George Marshall and the Class of 1901, at last the Kings of VMI, came back to school in September, returning for the last time. From the first day, cadets would often think or say, "This is the last time we have to . . ." do whatever it was they had to do. As First Classmen, they had plenty to do.

Marshall, Peyton, and Nicholson lived in Room 31, a double room, on the Second Stoop that year. Marshall always had a goal to reach. Being First Captain, he had no more rank to run for. That year he was "running" for zero demerits---- for all four years---- since he had received none for the first three years! George and Buster had a deal with Nick--- they did all the housekeeping of their room and Nick took any demerits their room received.

All the Firsts had certain privileges such as wearing their long gray capes lined with red, draped around their shoulders like a Roman toga, when they went into town. On weekday afternoons, they could leave the Post with merely reporting their going and returning to the O.D. and not have to apply in writing for permission to do so, as they did the years before. At all times, before class parades, company or battalion formations, First Class members only were allowed to gather around Washington's statue in front of the barracks. No other cadets were allowed to set foot on that sacred and forbidden spot.

Some privileges were valued more than others, and First Class privates enjoyed sleeping through that 6:20 a.m. reveille, or they could skip morning roll call and breakfast. Some ordered a Rat to bring them their breakfast to their room!

But whatever priveleges others had, Pug Marshall was at the top, he was the #1 cadet, he was the best.

As First Captain, one of his duties included commanding the battalion at the three daily mess hall formations and presiding over every meal. He had a special table in the center of the dining hall, and every now and then he would rise from his chair and demand, "Order in the Mess Hall!"

Henry Fry said, "He pronounced it, 'Mez-zall', because of his Pittsburgh twang, but nevertheless, it would get so quiet we could hear a pin drop."

Marshall was, "From start to finish, a most military First Captain. His sharp, crisp, commands could be clearly heard, and they demanded action," Henry Fry said.

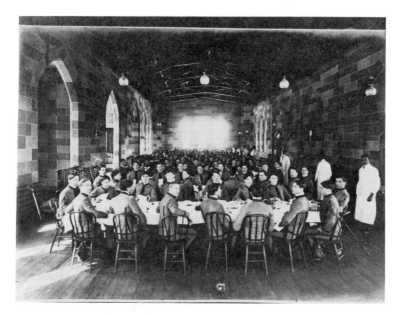

Once as the cadets were eating a wonderful, special dessert of fresh strawberries, a cadet tried his hand at imitating the First Captain and shushing the mess hall mumblings. Not knowing exactly who it was who was so brave, Marshall simply stood up, called the entire corps to attention, and marched them out of the dining hall.

About two thirds of their strawberries were left uneaten. Nobody tried that trick again, at least not on George C. Marshall.

"The impact of VMI on my later leadership was probably much greater than I realized at the time. . . I was responsible for the men, and you couldn't go to sleep on that. You had to know just what you were doing, and you had to have some talent in putting it over. . . Of course, if they could get away with anything, that was considered a good stunt and didn't particularly reflect on the cadet captain unless he was unable to manage it."

George Marshall had tried football during the year before, but didn't play much because of the Typhoid Furlough. In 1900, the football captain came looking for George and asked him to come out for practice. George had not thought to go out for football because he had so many military duties, but once they asked him, out he went. It was his last year and a last chance to play college football. He became a first string player and a fine left tackle.

The 1900 football season saw the best football team the Institute had ever put on the field. In their games, they held the University of Virginia to a 0-0 tie, defeated Virginia Polytechnic Institute (their arch rivals) 5-0 and G. Marshall got his name in the local paper for playing so well. They beat Washington & Lee twice--11-0 and 41-0.

George Marshall was named All Southern Conference Tackle in 1900. His injured arm must not have bothered him much, because he had a great and glorious football year.

One day as he walked back to the barracks from football practice, he passed by the house at the Limit Gates. Hearing a piano being played ever so sweetly, he stopped to listen. The song he heard was one his mother often played when he was a boy. He made an effort to be "just passing by" more than once, and he stopped often to listen. Once he was invited inside to meet the piano player, he was a goner! George C. Marshall fell in love.

Henry Fry wrote about it. "Early in First Class year, we heard astounding news. Purg Marshall was in love. The news was difficult to believe. He had never been known as a 'calic' man. Lily was a beautiful girl. She was tall, with dark hair, a lovely smile, and gorgeous eyes." She was a popular local beauty, known to everyone as Lily. George learned that she had dated many others, even his brother Stuart, but that made no difference. George was taking over.

George C. Marshall broke the rules! He risked certain demotion, "getting busted," and even getting expelled.. He "ran the block" for Elizabeth Carter Coles!

"Running the block", meant he left the barracks when he shouldn't have, fixed his pillows and blankets to make it look like he was in the bed, so that when 'bed check' was made, nobody could tell he wasn't already asleep.

His roommates, Nick and Buster, helped him by arranging a warning signal for him. If he heard their special whistle while he was at Lily's house, he jumped from her yard back onto VMI property pronto. He would slip back into his room and into safety. They always breathed easier once he was safely back in Room 31. Had he been caught, the famous First Captain could have been sent packing!

Marshall believed completely in VMI rules, but many years later, General Marshall said,

"I was very much in love and I was willing to take the chance."

George Marshall was an all-around VMI cadet, excelling in military and athletic ability, but he was not a brilliant student. At his graduation, he stood 15th in his class of thirty-three. George Marshall worked hard to learn, but some knowledge never came easily to him. Math was not his best field, but military studies were. His best subjects was Ordnance & Gunnery, where he was 6th out of thirty-four followed closely by his Civil Engineering ranking of 5th out of 18 and Military Science & Art of War, where he placed 8th out of thirty-four.

Henry Fry said, "Many times I have seen him in math class, standing at a blackboard with a mouth full of chalk trying to solve some problem that had him stumped."

George Marshall was one of the best cadet officers VMI has ever seen. With all of his military efficiency, he remained popular and well-liked because of his friendly disposition. He was a 'booster' of others, never having an unkind word to say about anyone.

He attained his last "running"---he finished all four years at VMI without any recorded demerits! Few cadets can make that claim, but there were five others in the class of 1901. The hardest thing George Marshall had to face during his last year of college was obtaining an army commission.

The United States Army was about three times as big as it had been before the Spanish-American War, so it needed more commissioned officers. West Point graduates had the edge over any other college graduates at being commissioned new lieutenants.

Next in line were those already in the army and ready for promotion, followed by officers of the Volunteers who wanted to enlist. Civilians came last. In the spring of 1901, there were 142 lieutenant vacancies and 10,000 applications on file.

It took a bit of doing to get George C. Marshall commissioned. His father wrote letters for him to important business friends and to congressmen, and Superintendent Shipp wrote a letter, on George's behalf, to President McKinley.

In April of 1901, George himself went to Washington, D.C. and visited several of his father's friends. Things were not looking hopeful so, as a last attempt, he made his way into the office of President McKinley, sneaking right in behind some other visitors!

When the President asked what he could do for him, George told him that he wished to be allowed to take the examination for a commission.

He went back to Lexington and waited. On June 17, he learned he would be allowed to take the examination in September. He could not be commissioned before January 1 of 1902, however, since he would not be 21 until December 31.

Would he ever have a life as a soldier? He didn't know in June of 1901. All he knew then was he had done the best he could. He would become an officer if he passed the examination and was given the chance. He was ready for the Army whenever the Army was ready for him.

Graduation Day for the 1901 Class was June 26th, and there was a continuous drizzle off and on all day. George C. Marshall did not receive a B.S. degree (Bachelor of Science) but only a diploma.

In 1901, and until 1912, only the highest ranking academic students, usually five or six, were awarded degrees. Out of the 122 Rats that had started in September of 1897, 33 graduated.

Years later, as his name made the news headlines again and again, during the 1940s and 50s, some of those cadets probably said to their children and grandchildren, "Hey! I remember Pug Marshall!"

In September of 1897, he had been the last cadet in his class to arrive, but he finished at the head of the military line. George had certainly not disgraced the family name at VMI as his brother had feared he would. In Uniontown, his parents accepted the fact that he wanted a career in the army, and he was engaged to marry Lily. He was last in the family, but he surely wasn't the least. He showed his brother Stuart a thing or two, he "wiped his eye" all right!

George C. Marshall wasn't a VMI cadet anymore. He was a VMI man!

He takes his place at the head of the great commanders of history."
- Harry S. Truman

George C. Marshall---Who In the World Was He?

Some people don't know about George C. Marshall. He was never our president or famous in sports or science, music or movies. All he did was enlist in the U.S. Army, serve in World Wars I and II, organize and direct the U.S. armed forces of World War II as the Army chief of staff, become the first U.S. five star general, serve as a special U.S. emissary to China, serve as president of the American Red Cross, be the first military man to serve as secretary of state, be the author of the Marshall Plan, serve as secretary of defense, and win the 1953 Nobel Prize for Peace . That wasn't much. It only took him fifty-one years.

George C. Marshall was probably like many other children of the late eighteen hundreds but, unlike most others, he became a true American hero of the nineteen hundreds. George C. Marshall served his country as both a soldier and a statesman.

After forty-three years of army service, Marshall had a civilian career as a special emissary to China, secretary of state, president of the American Red Cross, and secretary of defense. Because of his work on the European Recovery Plan, George C. Marshall became the first professional soldier to win the Nobel Prize for Peace.

But he never ran for president or any public office because he was not a politician. He never even voted. He felt that voting would be taking sides, and he said that he served all the people, not just one group. George C. Marshall did not seek personal power or high positions.

He was reserved, sometimes stern, yet he had a keen sense of humor, and always he was courteous. His appearance commanded respect. Even presidents called him General Marshall or Mr. Secretary, instead of George.

George C. Marshall could be severe, critical and stubborn, but he was fair, honest and sincere. He had integrity, a strong sense of duty, honor and country. He worked for America and not for himself.

The facts and stories of General Marshall's two careers, as soldier and statesman, might fill five books the size of this one. Here, you will find facts and stories only from his childhood, teen-age and college years. These were told by General Marshall to his official biographer, Forrest C. Pogue, who recorded them on tape and used them for references when he wrote his four books of General Marshall's life. Most of the quotations in this book are directly from George C. Marshall.

Will we have another American hero, one for a new century? Maybe today, in some classroom, someone like George Catlett Marshall is growing and learning. Maybe that someone is you.

"He is a patriot, a distinguished soldier, and the most selfless public servant I have ever met."

> *- Dwight David Eisenhower*

The Marshall Plan -
What In the World Was It?

In January of 1948, seven Cub Scouts from Bethesda, Maryland crowded around the Secretary of State as they explained their "Junior Marshall Plan" to him. They wanted his approval of their money-making scheme.

George C. Marshall listened to the Scouts' idea with interest and surprise. He was interested in learning what the young citizens were doing. And he was surprised they knew so much about the world situation.

At the end of World War II in 1945, many countries
and many people in Europe and Great Britain were in trouble.
Bombs and fighting had destroyed towns and cities, factories,
railroads, bridges and highways, hospitals, homes, schools
and churches. Their lives were very hard. Food, medicine,
clothing and shelter were scarce for families. City people could
not get raw materials or food from the farms. Farmers could
not get fuel, clothes, machinery or supplies from the cities.
And the governments had no money to help the people.

Boys and girls in America did not suffer because of the war, The United States was not bombed. Starvation, disease, and homelessness was not a problem for them in 1947.

During the years 1941-45, Army Chief-of-Staff George C. Marshall had been in Europe and had seen the action of war. In 1947, as Secretary of State, George C. Marshall visited Europe again. He saw the trouble, and he was worried. He felt that Western Europe and Great Britain would fall into more trouble as the Soviet Union tried to take over the ailing governments, offering help and bringing communism.

He and his staff began to talk about what the United States could do. World peace, democracy and economic prosperity were dependent on each other. George Marshall said that economic stability was necessary for political stability and without these factors, peace was not certain.

Marshall said America should have, ". . . a sense of responsibility for world order and security." He thought the United States should lead the way in stabilizing the economies of Western Europe and Britain. The U.S. could help to secure a lasting peace, and bring economic benefits to Europe and Britain and also to itself.

A strong method was needed that would give the countries help in money and materials while the people kept control of their own governments. Marshall enlisted the best of help to help develop a plan. He talked to his staff and to President Harry S. Truman.

After the plan was written, it was presented to the Congress as the Truman Doctrine. While Congress debated the policy, Marshall went to Moscow in March of 1947. The Big Four conference, with the foreign ministers of the Soviet Union, Britain, France and Secretary of State Marshall, met forty-four times during that month but could reach no agreement.

George C. Marshall became frustrated with long talks and no decisions. Even his own state department couldn't agree on what to do. Secretary Marshall and President Truman were in complete agreement. Several speeches were given, articles were written, and Congress seriously worked on the problem.

In June, George C. Marshall was invited to receive an honorary degree as part of the graduation ceremonies at Harvard University in Cambridge, Massachusetts. He accepted the degree and in return he gave a speech.

George C. Marshall was not noted for his speeches. He didn't like to speak to crowds and he did not have a strong voice. But on that June day, he made his most famous speech, and history was made.

"Our policy is directed not against any country or doctrine but against hunger, poverty, desperation and chaos."

Secretary of State George C. Marshall
at Harvard University
June 5, 1947

When the plan was presented to the full Congress, it was known as the European Recovery Plan. Congress agreed to back the program with financial help of over six million dollars for the first year beginning in April of 1948 if the different countries would develop their own solutions to solve their economic problems.

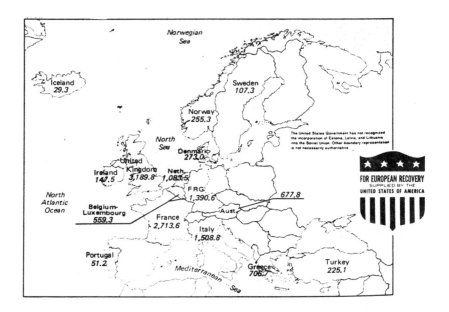

President Truman declared the policy should be named the Marshall Plan, in honor of the Secretary of State who had worked so long and hard. Congress appropriated more than 13 billion dollars through the Marshall Plan, and economic and material aid to the war-torn countries began in 1948.

The largest amounts went to Great Britain, France and Italy. Other countries accepting money and material products were Austria, Belgium, Denmark, Federal Republic of Germany, Greece, Iceland, Ireland, Luxembourg, Netherlands, Norway, Portugal, Sweden, Switzerland and Turkey.

In the war, Germany and Italy had been enemies of France and Belgium, as well as of the United States. The Marshall Plan helped the people to rebuild their industries and governments and begin again, in peace. The Soviet Union did not participate in giving or receiving aid through the Marshall Plan.

For their part, the Bethesda Cub Scouts would sponsor a movie for children and their parents. The profit from the movie went, by way of their "Junior Marshall Plan", to the poor children of Europe.

BENEFIT SHOW

ROY ROGERS
in "MY PAL TRIGGER"
and
CARTOONS

By Cub Pack 232
Boy Scouts of America, Bethesda, Md.,
For

Needy Children of Europe
ALL PROCEEDS TO CARE, Inc.

BETHESDA THEATER
FRIDAY, FEB. 13th 4 P. M.

ADULTS 50c   CHILDREN 25c
TAX INCLUDED

They asked for George C. Marshall's approval and support to help them advertize. And they got it! They also got an off-the-cuff speech complimenting them on their awareness of the world situation and of the seriousness of the situation in Europe.

George C. Marshall was very fond of children. He sometimes preferred talking to them than to adults. He told the Cubs a few stories of how little he knew of geography and of other cultures at their age of nine and ten, and of how modern communication was making information easier to obtain. They were lucky compared to himself at age ten. He congratulated them on their efforts and wished them well.

"I wish very much that I could have had something like this in my record as a boy."

"I think it is so impressive for a group of boys of your age to undertake to provide food for a year for a number of starving children in Europe. It is a generous and a fine action on your part for those children who are in dire need of such help. And it (the Marshall Plan) is of real international importance to this government in establishing a basis of friendship and good will and trust that is so important to our people, and to the world and to peace."

George C. Marshall received the Nobel Prize for Peace in 1953.

98

IMPORTANT TIMES IN THE
LIFE OF GEORGE C. MARSHALL

December 31, 1880 — Born in Uniontown, Pennsylvania

September 1897-June 1901—Attended Virginia Military Institute

February 3, 1902—Commissioned 2nd Lieutenant, U.S. Army

February 11, 1902—Married Elizabeth ("Lily") Carter Coles

April 1919—Aide-de-camp of General "Black Jack " Pershing

September 15, 1927—Elizabeth Coles "Lily" Marshall died

October 15, 1930—Married Katherine Tupper Brown

August 24, 1936—Attained rank of brigadier general

September 1, 1939—Appointed Chief of Staff of the U. S. Army

December 1944—Became first U.S. five-star general

January 21, 1947—Named Secretary of State

June 5, 1947—Marshall Plan speech at Harvard

1949-1950—President of the American Red Cross

September 14, 1950—Named Secretary of Defense

June 1953—Chairman, U.S. Delegation to the Coronation of Queen Elizabeth II

December 10, 1953—Received the Nobel Prize for Peace

October 16, 1959—Died at Walter Reed Army Hospital, Washington, D.C. Buried in Arlington National Cemetery

BIBLIOGRAPHY

Bland, Larry I. and Sharon Ritenour Stevens, eds. The Papers of George Catlett Marshall. Volume 1. Baltimore. Johns Hopkins University Press. 1981.

Bland, Larry I., and Joellen K. Bland, eds. George C. Marshall Interviews and Reminiscences for Forrest C. Pogue, Revised ed. Lexington, Va.: George C. Marshall Foundation. 1991.

Davis, Thomas W., ed. A Crowd of Honorable Youths: Historical Essays on the First 150 Years of the Virginia Military Institute. Lexington, Va. VMI Sesquicentennial Committee. 1988.

Frye, William. Marshall--Citizen Solider. The Bobbs-Merrill Company. New York. 1947.

Fry, Henry. Memories of the Old VMI, Volumes I - IV. (Unpublished) Virginia Military Archives. 1930.

Mosley, Leonard. Marshall: Hero for Our Times. New York. Hearst Books. 1982.

Payne, Robert. The Marshall Story, a Biography of General George C. Marshall. Prentice-Hall. New York. 1951.

Pogue, Forrest C. George C. Marshall, Education of a General 1880-1939. New York: The Viking Press, 1963.

Stoler, Mark A. George C. Marshall, Soldier-Statesman of the American Century. Boston. Twayne Publishers. 1989.

Story, Walter "Buzz". Uniontown, Stories of Uniontown and Fayette County. Sponsored by Mr. and Mrs. Robert E. Epley and Uniontown Newspapers, Inc. 1993.

The George C. Marshall Foundation. "Fully the Equal of the Best" George C. Marshall and the Virginia Military Institute. Lexington, Virginia.1996./p

NOTES

The inside covers display a map of the Baltimore & Ohio railroad from the late eighteen hundreds and was loaned to the author by George N. Johnson, Jr. of Lexington, Virginia. You can trace the route George Marshall might have taken if riding the train from Uniontown to Lexington.

Photographs for this book are from the George C. Marshall Library and the Virginia Military Institute Archives in Lexington, Virginia.

The maps of Uniontown, the Historic National Road, and Fayette County were used with the editor's permission from the collected news stories, Uniontown, edited by Walter "Buzz" Storey.

The Cub Scouts featured in the newspaper clipping may see this book and be surprised. Three of them were contacted by the author. Robert K. Linden contributed the copy of the movie poster featured in the Marshall Plan section.

Quotations in the story come from George C. Marshall's tape recorded comments given to his biographer, Forrest C. Pogue, and written in the book Interviews and Reminiscences. Some quotes are from Henry Fry as he wrote them in his memoirs. He was a VMI classmate of Marshall's and a member of the year book staff. Several other quotes are credited elsewhere.

The cover design was created by Jeanne Pedersen, Director of Publication at the George C. Marshall Foundation in Lexington.

The front cover photo comes from a group photo of George C. Marshall and some of his best friends, including Herb Bowman, one of George's bee fighting buddies. The picture was donated to the Marshall Museum by Dr. and Mrs. John B. Blakley, of Allison Park, Pennsylvania and relatives of Herbert Bowman.

101